YOUR FAITH / YOUR COMM

confirm

MENTOR GUIDE

APPROVED UNITED METHODIST CONFIRMATION

Confirm Mentor Guide
Your Faith. Your Commitment. God's Call.

Writer: Teri Chalker

Contents

Meet the Writer

Teri Chalker holds a social work degree from the University of Kansas and a master's degree in social work from Southern Illinois University Carbondale. She worked in the medical field until she began serving on staff at Church of the Resurrection's Leawood Campus in 2003. Beginning as the elementary program director, Teri transitioned to her current role as the director of WILD1's (a fifth-grade youth group) and Confirmation. Teri has been the director of confirmation for the past nine years. She also serves as a coach for the Youth Ministry Institute.

Introduction

I remember over ten years ago when I decided to take on my new role of directing our church's confirmation program. I was looking for a change and something to challenge me. I started the position at the end of October, and the confirmation ceremony was in November. I immediately began planning, organizing, and preparing for the conclusion of the journey I had jumped into. However, nothing could prepare my heart emotionally for the ministry into which I was about to pour my heart. I sat in the front row of that confirmation ceremony and watched as young people I knew from working in previous years as the elementary program director bowed at kneelers. Standing behind them were the families I had grown to love, and in front of the teens stood their mentors laying their hands on and praying for the young people they had been guiding over the weeks.

Tears were flowing that day—even from the eyes of "tough" male mentors. One of them shared that as he looked into the eyes of the confirmands and the parents' tearful proud faces, it was almost impossible to not feel such strong emotions. This was the feeling of the powerful moving of the Holy Spirit.

I pretty much cried almost the entire first confirmation ceremony I directed. I remember walking up to our senior pastor at the reception afterwards and telling him they made a mistake hiring me for this position as I cried the whole ceremony. I will never forget what he said back to me: "Teri, I think we hired the exact right person."

Confirmation is as much about the changing of one's heart as it is the changing of one's head. There is something so very powerful to see young people have the courage to stand in front of family, friends, and church family and profess that they want to be followers of Jesus Christ. This is the journey that you as a mentor are getting ready to take part in. It's an adventure that you and the teenagers you will be mentoring will get to be on with God leading you the entire way. So hang on, what a ride it will be!

The confirmation journey not only changes a young person's life, but it also changes the family's as well. Even more so, I can promise, you will be impacted. Mentors often say, "I knew the teens were going to grow in confirmation, but I had no idea how much I would grow in my faith."

Now that you have decided to mentor, these may be some of your fears:

- "How will I find time in my own busy life to meet with a young person every week?"

- "They are not going to want to hang out with me. I'm not cool enough."

- "I don't know enough about the Bible to be a mentor."

- "What if we have nothing to talk about?"

If it makes you feel any better, you are not the only one asking these questions. The purpose of this mentor guide is to help address them, to let you know you are not alone, and to help you feel encouraged, supported, and equipped to embark on one of the most important journeys of a young person's life — the confirmation journey. Just know that you have been called to do this. Jesus will equip you for what lies ahead.

> I'm sure about this: the one who started a good work in you will stay with you to complete the job by the day of Christ Jesus. (Philippians 1:6)

1 *What Is Confirmation?*

I sometimes forget in my director role when I'm in the midst of signing teenagers up, making lesson plans, recruiting volunteers, and developing the schedule that confirmation is much more than just the details. The families we serve look at confirmation as a life event—a rite of passage. I remember a teen whose mom died of cancer two years prior to her getting confirmed and she left small gifts with handwritten notes for the things she considered life events—her graduation from high school, her graduation from college, her marriage, and the birth of her first child AND she left one for confirmation. For this mom to think about her confirmation two years prior to her daughter going though it is so telling. I carry this story with me as a good reminder of the significance of the life event that confirmation is for our young people and for all of us who get to be part of it.

Confirmation is as much about the changing of one's heart as it is the changing of one's head.

The word *confirm* means "to make (something) stronger or more certain : to cause (someone) to believe (something) more strongly."[1] In the act of confirmation, a young person is therefore confirming or making his or her faith stronger. Confirmation should be about not just what is learned but also how it is learned.

Confirmation has been around for a long time. The various ways it has been practiced reflect the rich heritages of each denomination that has used it to teach their young the Christian faith. A comprehensive overview of confirmation's history is found in the *Confirm Director Guide*.

Each young person's confirmation journey will be as different and unique as the individual. Parents, teenagers, and even mentors stand at the threshold of the confirmation process bringing their own unique experiences and stories to enhance the experience for each confirmand.

As you begin your church's confirmation journey, keep in mind that how young people learn and grow in faith today is not the same as when you were young. Confirmation should be interactive, experiential, and fun! It needs to be a place where the young people can discover who Jesus is to them and what faith looks like in their lives. This is where your role as a mentor is vital. You will guide and lead them on this discovery. Coming to know who Jesus is and professing faith in him should be personal and unique for each person. Having a mentor who knows them and understands them will help them make the connection between faith and life during this confirmation journey.

The church's attitude about confirmation has also changed. There was a time when it seemed to be focused on getting members and checking confirmation off the "to do" list. The church is now starting to realize that confirmation can be so much more. We can shake things up and make the confirmation experience something more—the foundation to a lifetime of discipleship.

This movement into making confirmation more than a set of classes began as churches realized they were confirming young people and then never seeing them again in the life of the church. Getting teens confirmed is the easy part. Keeping them engaged and growing in a faith that will stick is the hard part. Fortunately, churches are now asking, "How can we change our programming to promote a young person's desire to follow Jesus and remain a part of this person's church community and the body of Christ?"

There are many things we can do to make the process more engaging, such as using interactive curriculum, partnering with parents, and connecting our teens with church as a

Confirm Mentor Guide

whole. However, arguably the most effective components to keep teens engaged with your faith community after the confirmation ceremony are the relationships they make on the journey. One of these relationships is the one they will have with you. Caring, kind, and compassionate adults who gently guide and hold young people accountable are critical to their ongoing participation in the life of the church. We will talk more about the roles of mentors later in this book.

Confirmation leaders and those who write curriculum know that not only do teenagers need to know Christian theology, learn the nature of the church, and explore their faith commitments, but they also need to find ways to integrate all of it into their everyday lives. Our job is not to tell them who God is and what to believe, but instead to help them discover who God is and grow to trust God with their lives.

Confirmation is not a set of classes to complete; it is more about relationships that teens build with family, church, and their God.

We need to communicate to teens that while confirmation concludes with a ceremony where they publicly proclaim their faith, confirmation is just a step on their faith journey, a journey they will be on with God their whole lives. Confirmation is not a set of classes to complete; it is more about relationships that teens build with family, church, and their God.

Confirmation and Baptism

Confirmation and baptism are inextricably connected. The United Methodist Church celebrates baptism and Communion as the only two sacraments. In The United Methodist Church, confirmands are to be baptized before they are confirmed. Many confirmands are baptized as babies. In that sacramental ceremony, the community of faith claims for a child God's promise of salvation, the child's parents promise to raise their child in the Christian faith, and the congregation promises to support the parents and share in that responsibility. Each teen baptized as a child who chooses to complete confirmation declares for herself or himself trust in Christ, thereby embracing God's promise of salvation made in baptism.

Often there are a number of confirmands who were not baptized as infants. Your congregation may baptize those teens as part of the confirmation ceremony or in a separate ceremony, as we do at Church of the Resurrection. Fellow confirmands, many of whom who were baptized as infants, their families, their mentors, and their families are all invited to support the confirmand being baptized. We've found that this experience of mentors and families laying hands on and praying for each confirmand being baptized is a meaningful way to mark and remember the baptisms and faith commitments. The support by all involved demonstrates in a very tangible way what it means to be the body of Christ.

Program Scheduling

One thing we've learned in confirmation is that the only constant in confirmation programs among United Methodist churches is that every church runs its confirmation program differently. Some programs run for ten weeks while others will run for two years. Scheduling the confirmation process for each church should be based on how the time frame fits into the life of the church and the community.

While the length of time a confirmation program runs is important, the No. 1 question asked by churches and families alike is, "What age should a young person go through confirmation?" The United Methodist Church website says that in many United Methodist congregations, preparation for confirmation begins when young people enter middle school years (sixth to eighth grades). This stage (referred to as early adolescence) is when young people begin to move from concrete thinking to abstract thinking. In other words, our young teens are beginning to practice their new ability to think beyond the facts. They now can reflect more deeply on ideas and concepts and what they mean. This is a prime time to engage young teens in deeper faith reflection and what it means to integrate faith learning into everyday life. Ultimately, we want our confirmands to be able to discern what following Jesus looks like in every situation and every environment— family, school, friends, sports team, and so forth. Helping your confirmand understand how confirmation class learning matters in his or her life is a critical role you have as a mentor.

Opinions vary over which of these grades a church should hold a confirmation class. It is up to each church to determine what is appropriate for their young people. That decision depends largely on your congregation, your community, and the leading of the Holy Spirit. To illustrate, my church's confirmation class lasts for one school year. We changed the program a few years ago from holding it for seventh-graders to holding it for those starting in eighth grade. We made the switch because we looked at our community. In our area, when a student moves into the eighth grade, practices, games, and other school activities take place during the week. Since confirmation meets on Sundays, switching to eighth grade made sense to avoid many sports conflicts that we were having with our seventh-grade students whose sports activities took place on the weekends. The classes are usually 80 percent eighth-graders while the rest are high school age—allowing for young people who come to the church after the typical confirmation year to also participate.

Scheduling to reduce potential calendar conflicts with confirmands and their families applies to the mentoring relationship as well. Setting meeting times and locations that integrate into their families' normal life rhythms not only sets you up for an effective mentoring relationship, but it also can support your effort to help your confirmand begin to make real world faith connections.

Requirements and Expectations

Nothing can derail a young person's confirmation experience faster than an adult who drops out partway through the process. Be sure you are clear on what is being asked of you. How long does the process last? Are you expected to attend the class? How many times are you expected to meet with your confirmand? What special activities are you expected to attend? Clarity on expectations of the program will put everyone involved on the same path. It is important not only to be aware of the expectations but also to determine if you have the capacity to fulfill the mentor responsibilities. It is perfectly acceptable to decline a mentor role in the present and return a year later when life situations are more amendable.

Since you will be holding your teen accountable, it's going to be important for you to understand what he or she is required to do as part of confirmation. For example, at Church of the Resurrection in Leawood, Kansas, our confirmation students' requirements to get confirmed are:

- They must attend the kickoff, retreat, and ceremony. The kickoff is attended by at least one other family member as well. The retreat is on a Friday night. Our ceremony is on a Sunday.

- They can not miss more than four sessions. This expectation is not meant as a "punishment" but instead as the reality that with only so many sessions, if the participant misses more than four, then that individual has missed a large percentage of the material presented each week. By missing a large amount of sessions, the church community connections that form between peers are greatly impacted.

Part of being a Christian is serving others, and confirmation is a way to teach the young people what it means to be a Christian.

- They must be baptized. All forms are recognized.

- They must take part in a mission. Part of being a Christian means serving others, and confirmation is a way to teach the young people what it means to be a Christian. We offer many places they can go with their mentor and serve. Mentors report that serving alongside their confirmands is one of their favorite things they do with their confirmands. You may even want to do it more than once. Make sure not only to serve but also to spend time talking about the experience afterwards. Reinforce it with Scripture such as Matthew 6:10 (ESV): "Your kingdom come, your will be done, on earth as it is in heaven."

- They must serve as an acolyte or usher four times. Serving in this way reinforces the connection with the church. Making confirmation visible to the church community is important. Confirmation should not be isolated from the life of the church.

- They need to be active in another area of the church such as attending youth group, Sunday school, or volunteering as an usher or in the nursery. This connection is something our mentors help them to find if they need it. The goal is not to make them busier but to connect them within the life of the church so that after confirmation is over someone will "miss them" if they start to fall away from church.

Commitment

Each family should consider the needs of their son or daughter to determine if their young person is ready for confirmation. Readiness is about the heart and head but also about priorities and schedule. Each family will need to consider how they will reprioritize sports and other commitments in order for their daughter or son to participate in the confirmation process. It is OK if that commitment cannot be made at the present. The opportunity to wait until they can commit to the time should be offered.

At Church of the Resurrection we take commitment seriously with grace. For example, a young person who starts the program and then finds he can't meet all the participation requirements is given the option to drop out and restart the following year. If a young person has fulfilled all the requirements but can't attend the mandatory retreat, she has the option to attend just the retreat and ceremony the following year.

We encourage every family to come and talk with us when conflicts arise or when they are considering whether to even start the confirmation process. Often, the mentor is the first person the family talks with. The best thing you can do to help them determine the best path forward is to facilitate a conversation with the confirmation director or pastor where options can be explored.

Finally, it is helpful for both you and your confirmand to set expectations for your time together. Negotiating what you both hope to give and gain from the relationship you are building can help calm your teen's anxiety, empower her or him, and set the tone for building trust. Remember, your job is not to get your confirmand to the finish line. Your job is to be an adult spiritual companion along his or her journey, listening, addressing questions, and encouraging the teen's family—whether the journey leads to the choice to confirm one's faith or to wait.

Chapter 1 Notes

1. From entry on "confirm," Merriam-Webster website, *merriam-webster.com/dictionary/confirm*. Accessed 23 August 2016.

2 What Is My Role As a Mentor?

Now that you have heard what confirmation is, you may be wondering how you as a mentor fit in on this journey. I always tell my mentors, "I am not looking for someone who knows all the answers, but instead someone who is willing to help a young person discover their own." Think of yourself as a guide, an encourager, a cheerleader, and a coach—all packaged into one for your young person!

Think of yourself as a guide, an encourager, a cheerleader, and a coach—all packaged into one for your young person!

Mentoring effectively is not about age or experience but about impact. Church of the Resurrection confirmation mentors include young adults, parents, and grandparents who have deeply and positively influenced the lives and faith of confirmands. We also enlist high school students who have been confirmed to serve as junior mentors. These young people serve alongside an adult mentor and can be as effective as an adult mentor.

If your confirmation program does not include junior mentors, I recommend giving it consideration. There is much to learn from these young people. Confirmands can relate to junior mentors in unique ways as they are closer in age and understand the young confirmand's life issues and experience. The junior mentors also serve as role models beyond the church when confirmands interact with them in the community. The message is pretty simple: you can be an impactful mentor at any age.

Mentorship is more about sharing and showing than it is about telling.

Who Can Be a Mentor?

A mentor is someone who is authentic. We've been told by our confirmands that the most effective mentor is not someone who tries to act like he or she is the confirmand's age, but instead is genuine in her or his actions and words. An authentic mentor is in tune to the needs of the young person he or she is mentoring without trying too hard to "relate." Rather, the effective mentor is able to demonstrate trustworthiness simply by being himself or herself and consistently modeling faith to the teen through actions and words. Passing on faith through a mentoring relationship is most effective when the confirmand observes the life of the mentor to be consistent with what he or she professes to believe.

A mentor is committed. One way to model to the confirmand that you are committed is to also follow confirmand requirements. For instance, if confirmands are allowed to miss only four classes over the confirmation year, then mentors should be held to the same expectations. By following the same requirements and expectations as the confirmand, the mentor is showing commitment to the church, the process, and the confirmand. Additionally, it shows the confirmand that this is important.

Other ways to model for your confirmand may involve asking yourself a few questions. As a mentor, are you participating in worship regularly? Studying Scripture? Praying and serving others? Your teen is watching you and will model your behavior.

A mentor is dedicated. Investing time in your teen's life will be important to him or her. Our mentors attend sporting events of their students and go to band concerts, plays, and other activities in which they are involved. The mentors attend funerals and write notes of encouragement or send cards for times when their teens need some encouragement and prayer. We believe that quantity is necessary for quality.

16

The importance of the bonds forged with the confirmand through the quantity of time spent together cannot be overstated. A couple of years ago we had a confirmand die tragically during the class. His mentors and a small group of boys not only attended the funeral together but also set up a mission project in his honor. Kind, caring mentors were able to effectively guide their confirmands through the grieving process because they spent time with them and knew them.

Mentors take ownership to think "outside the box." A good example of this characteristic is how one of our mentors likes to start his sessions. Understanding the unique needs of middle school boys, he takes his confirmand outside where they play catch. His confirmand can focus more easily after a short time of physical activity. Additionally, this serves as a way for them to connect in a natural way.

> **The importance of the bonds forged with the confirmand through the quantity of time spent together cannot be overstated.**

Another of our mentors set up a bar-b-que in the church parking lot and talked to the young people about how different rubs and seasons can make the meat taste differently, demonstrating how individuals bring their own "flavors" and "seasonings" to the body of Christ. This was not only a creative but also a yummy way to bring a point across and one the young people will never forget. So as a mentor you will have certain things you need to cover each week, but don't be afraid to try new things and use your creativity to bring learning to life.

Mentors are disciple makers. What is a disciple? When most of us think of the word *disciple*, we think of Jesus and his twelve disciples. Though many years have passed since these disciples were "recruited" to walk with Jesus, the work remains the same. "Therefore, go and make disciples of all nations, baptizing them in the name of the Father and of the Son and of the Holy Spirit" (Matthew 28:19). Jesus is asking you to disciple his students.

You may not realize it, but you were also recruited by Jesus to do his work. We are to be his hands and feet. "Then Jesus said to his disciples, 'All who want to come after me must say no to themselves, take up their cross, and follow me" (Matthew 16:24). Jesus is asking you to serve as a modern-day disciple. He is asking you to "Come, follow me, . . . and I'll show you how to fish for people" (Matthew 4:19). You are not only helping to impact a young person's faith journey, but you are also growing the body of Christ. You are fulfilling the Great Commission (Matthew 28:19).

You are helping to not only impact a young person's faith journey, but you are growing the body of Christ.

By saying yes to being a mentor, you are taking up his cross. You are agreeing to "let your light shine before people, so they can see the good things you do and praise your Father who is in heaven" (Matthew 5:16). Through you, your young person will see Jesus' light shine.

Why Are Mentors Important?

Now that you know that a mentor serves as a disciple of Jesus, you might be asking yourself why a mentor is important in the confirmation process. Before we get into that, let's look at how others influence the young person's experience as well.

Some churches' confirmation programs are run by a pastor, youth director, or confirmation director. These roles are important to the confirmand because they are the people who put all the aspects of the program together, including the lessons. They are a resource for you as a mentor for support, encouragement, and answers to your questions along the way.

A confirmand's family is important in the process because they have more time with the confirmand than anyone else in the process. The extra time creates opportunity to influence this son's or daughter's confirmation journey by demonstrating how to live out faith in daily real-life examples.

Finally, a confirmand's peers serve as encouragers and create a sense of belonging.

As a mentor, you are the person to whom the teen can go with questions about what the teen is learning. The young person will have a relationship with you that can be unique and tailored to the teen's own individual needs. You will be able to help the teen take what he or she is learning in the large group time and make it meaningful for his or her life. We tell our mentors, "We want you to walk beside your teen. We want your involvement with your teen to not be for just a defined amount of time (example: number of weeks the confirmation program runs), but rather for a lifetime. Please don't go into this relationship with the idea that it ends once the confirmation class has ended."

Confirmation should not be viewed as a graduation but instead as an important step in a lifelong process.

Confirmation should not be viewed as a graduation but instead as an important step in a lifelong process of following Jesus. My hope is that as a mentor you will be at your young person's graduation from high school, at his or her wedding, at the birth of the first child, and at this person's side when someone important in life is lost. I hope you hear in all of this that you have permission to not just mentor during the confirmation class but to become part of your confirmand's family as someone he or she can always go to with questions about life and faith.

For confirmation to serve the best interest of each young person and have its greatest impact, a team of committed adults working in concert is needed. When the resources and influences of the confirmation leader, family, peers, and mentor converge on behalf of each young person's confirmation journey, the young people are in the best possible situation to make faith commitments that last. Thank you for being on the team!

3 Creating a Safe Environment

Now that you understand what confirmation is and what your role in the journey is, let's explore how to keep not only your young person safe but yourself as well. This is always a tough topic to talk about with new mentors. It's hard not to take it personally when someone asks you to provide references and checks into your background. It can make you feel as though they don't trust you. As a mentor, you need to understand that churches put necessary processes and guidelines in place, not to be intrusive but in order to create a safe environment for both your confirmand and you.

Safe Sanctuaries®

In today's society, it is critical that churches take seriously the importance of providing a safe environment where all people can participate freely and safely in the life of the church. Safe Sanctuaries® is one way The United Methodist Church works toward maintaining a "safe place" for all to grow in faith and maturity. The Safe Sanctuaries® program certifies volunteers, staff, and clergy in boundary awareness and abuse prevention as "an overt expression in making congregations safe places where children, youth, and elders may experience the abiding love of God and fellowship within the community of faith."[1]

Churches take seriously the importance of providing a safe environment where all people can participate freely and safely in the life of the church.

As a mentor, you need to know that it's not just your home church that is asking you to provide information and go through a process to get certified. All United Methodist churches are strongly encouraged to establish a Safe Sanctuaries® policy for everyone working with children and youth in any event or activity sponsored by your local church. If your church does not have a Safe Sanctuaries® policy and your children and youth ministry workers have not been trained in it, talk to your church staff about how to begin policy-making, training, and the certification process. More information can be found at *umcdiscipleship.org*.

If you need to be trained before your church has the opportunity to establish its policy, the education and certification process for Safe Sanctuaries® can be done online through the *umcdiscipleship.org* website. The information you will get by taking this class online will help direct and guide you as you begin to meet with your young person and have confidence knowing you are creating a safe environment for you both to have a healthy and growing relationship. State and national background checks will need to be completed for each applicant. Your conference can provide direction on how to have them done. While this process will take you some time and work to get safe sanctuary certified, it is critical to complete before you begin.

Rules for a Healthy Relationship

In light of Safe Sanctuaries® there are some basic rules and guidelines you should use when meeting with your teenager. While some of these may seem inhibiting, they are important. The following guidelines will make both you and your young person feel more comfortable in growing your relationship in a healthy way. While Safe Sanctuaries® is a certification you complete, these guidelines below serve as practical ways to implement what you learned in Safe Sanctuaries® training into your meeting times. Here are some "rules" to help you develop strong and healthy ministry relationships with the young people you work with:

- Always have two unrelated adults in every setting if possible. If not, make sure and always meet with an individual young person in an open, public area where there are other people in line of sight—such as a coffee shop or narthex of your church. Never be alone in a building, home, car, or any private area with a young person. While this might seem limiting, by abiding by this rule you are keeping your chance of someone saying something happened that didn't to a lower risk.

- Do not drive alone with a young person. If transporting teenagers in your personal car, you should have one other unrelated adult in the car with you.

- Make sure your young person's parents or church staff know that you are meeting with the individual. A simple e-mail or text to a teenager's family or church staff will work. You can even just "cc" or add them to the communication you have with your young person so you do not have to send out separate e-mails.

- Young people utilize technology as a primary source of communication, but as an adult, be careful when using it to communicate with your teenager. While it can serve to enhance your relationships through text messages, Facebook, Twitter, and so forth, you should not use it as your primary way to grow your relationship. Some conversations need to take place off-line—like disagreements or sensitive topics. When you talk online, there is no eye contact or facial expressions. These nonverbal cues help reinforce what you were trying to communicate. There is a possibility your teenager can "misread" what you were actually trying to say.

- Whether you choose to communicate with your teenager in handwritten notes, cards, or electronic communication such as Facebook or text messages, use care and wisdom. Leave no room for question in the topics or words you use, especially with electronic communication. A good rule of thumb is to use it only to communicate information and save conversation for face-to-face time.

- While you may come from a home environment where things like hugging are natural, when working with your young person be mindful that although physical affection can have an appropriate place in ministry, you should use discretion. Avoid inappropriate touch, including massages. Hugging should be from the side only, and never without permission. Giving high fives or fist bumps are great ways to show affection. It should go without saying that kissing of any sort is inappropriate.

- Any physical contact should be in response to the need of the young person and not the need of the adult and generally in response to a young person's initiative. Each young person is very different. Some will run up and want to hug you every time they meet you. Others won't even look you in the face when you are talking to them. As you get to know your confirmand, follow their lead.

- Physical restraint should be used only in order to protect the health and welfare of the young person, other young people, volunteers, or staff and according to church policy.

- Some teens you meet with might be going through some difficult times in their home or school life. They may be seeking an adult who can "save" them from these difficulties. While your heart might want to help them in any way possible, resist the temptation to overstep the boundary of a mentor to become a savior. We are here to introduce them to Jesus their Savior and help them develop a relationship with him. For long-term difficulties or issues in the confirmand's life, talk it

We are here to introduce them to Jesus their Savior.

over with your youth director or pastor to get advice on how to proceed.

- Avoid lengthy amounts of time "counseling" teenagers. Young people who need counseling should be referred to someone who is a counselor, and the appropriate church staff should be consulted and notified.

- You are an example to teenagers in every way. For that reason, be mindful and modest in your dress, behavior, language, body language, and social media. Be conscious of how your appearance will speak to both genders. High standards should be followed not only inside the walls of the church but also outside in the community as well. Whether you are at a grocery store or sporting events, remember you are role models for your young person.

- In order to establish trust with your teen, confidentiality is vital. Never discuss what a teen says to you with other parents or teens. A young person will stop sharing if they hear from someone else something private they told you in one of your meetings together.

- While you want to establish confidentiality with your confirmand, you should never promise a young person that you will not share with others something the young person shares with you. If a teenager says to you, "If I tell you something, do you promise not to tell anyone else?," you need to tell the teen that while you want to respect his or her privacy, you will need to tell someone if the teen shares he or she is going to harm himself or herself or someone else. If your teen does share that he or she has these thoughts, then you need to let your church staff know immediately. They will follow up with the teen and family. A thorough Safe Sanctuaries® policy will include the process and people you can go to with safety concerns.

Legal Responsibility

Know your legal responsibility. Currently, in twenty-eight states, clergy members and those involved in the care of children and youth are considered "mandated reporters," meaning you have a specific obligation to report suspected child abuse or neglect. Updated information on these mandates in your particular state can be found at Child Welfare Information Gateway at *childwelfare.gov*. If your young person shares any physical abuse or neglect with you, you will also need to report this to church staff.

Remember that guidelines and rules are set to protect you as well as young people. It is understandable that these guidelines must be subject to grace and the promptings of the Holy Spirit. If you feel you need adjustment to these guidelines, you should talk to your appropriate church staff.

Chapter 3 Notes

1. "Safe Sanctuaries," Discipleship Ministries of The United Methodist Church website, *umcdiscipleship.org/leadership-resources/safe-sanctuaries*. Accessed 11 October 2016.

4 Relationships That Last

Now that we have looked at some ways to create healthy and safe relationships, let's explore ways to make your relationship last. As we discussed previously, confirmation programs are changing. Churches are realizing that while learning fundamentals of the Christian faith are important, it's really the relationships the confirmands make while in confirmation that contribute most to a faith that lasts.

As a director, I have been feeling the Holy Spirit nudging me to make relationship building a greater emphasis in our confirmation program. It really hit home for me when one former mentor said to me that she wished she had stayed connected with her confirmands after confirmation was over. When I asked her why she didn't, she said, "Because no one ever asked me to." My heart dropped. Really? All I had to do was ask the mentors to consider staying in a relationship with their confirmands and they would. I now make it a point when I meet with mentors to present to them the vision of creating a long-term relationship with their confirmands. Below we will present some ways to help grow your mentoring relationship.

All I had to do was ask the mentors to consider staying in a relationship with their confirmands and they would.

The following tips are geared toward one to one mentoring because it is the most common approach. However, they are certainly transferable to group mentoring, which is what we do at the United Methodist Church of the Resurrection. Later we'll talk specifically about why group mentoring has its benefits.

Tips to Growing Your Relationship

- Hopefully, you will have freedom to think about your meeting space. How comfortable a space is it to have a conversation? Will you meet at the church building or offsite (coffee shop or other building)? Think about the setting (chairs, lighting, location, and so forth). We find in our ministry that sitting at tables make young people feel they are in school. Having a table between you and your teen can create a physical divide. While a classroom might be good for a teaching session, your role with your teen is to grow relationally. So you will want to find a place where you can sit comfortably next to each other and not create a teacher/student type feeling by talking across a table. We find that when given a choice between couches in the hallway or a classroom with table and chairs, most mentors and young people will choose the couches.

- As a mentor, when thinking of your meeting place, you will also want to see if there will be a lot of other young people the same age as your confirmand at this location because they may feel reluctant to "be seen" with you. At their age, young people are inhibited by the fact that others may be watching them. Most don't want to stand out or appear different. So finding somewhere they can feel they can be themselves is important in helping them relax and feel comfortable enough to open up and share. Your choice of meeting space will set the tone.

- Remove technology distractions, such as cell phones, during your time together. This includes your phone as well.

- Be consistent and reliable in your meeting times. With cell phones there really is no reason not to let a young person know if you are running late or if an emergency comes up. However, don't make this a habit. Young people will count on you to be where you say you are going to be, and when. Dependability is a significant part of developing a sense of trust in your relationship. You will be setting the example to them about making your meetings a priority. If you show them it's important to you, then they too will feel the meetings are important.

- To help with consistency and demonstrate accountability, consider using the Meeting Tracker resource at the end of this guide. You can use the tracker to record dates, location, times, and highlights from your meetings with your confirmand. Keeping track of these key meeting details is also a great way to help you focus your discussions for the next time you meet and remind yourself of any issues or questions you might need to research for the next meeting.

Dependability is a significant part of developing a sense of trust in your relationship.

- Since most of your teenagers will be driven by a family member to meet with you—and we know families are very busy—it's important to begin and end each session on time. Ending on time shows the teen's family that you value their time as well.

- While some young people interact with adults naturally, others may take time to adjust to this new relationship. Just like you might be a new mentor, your young person most likely hasn't experienced a mentoring relationship before either. So allow your young person time to figure out how to navigate and participate in your developing relationship. You will need to guide him or her along the way. At the onset, explain that this is a learning relationship. You are not the teen's teacher but a guide, encourager, and friend. Set some ground

You are not the teen's teacher but a guide, encourager, and friend.

rules for your time together and your expectations of your teen's involvement. Make sure and ask her what she expects of you as well. Ask what he hopes to gain from your time together. Put all of this in writing so that you both can keep the direction you hope to go in front of you throughout the confirmation process.

• You can help alleviate initial nervousness starting your first meeting by sharing about yourself. Share why you chose to be a mentor. Tell any fears or thoughts you are having about this confirmation journey you will be on together. Share how you came to be a Christ follower or believer with your young person—not just the surface details, but also the deep stuff. Share any struggles you might have had along the way with your faith, as appropriate. Knowing where you are coming from is important in establishing a trusting relationship with your young person. It also creates an environment where he or she can feel comfortable sharing fears and struggles with you.

Be ready for wherever your teenager is on his or her faith walk.

• Be ready for wherever your teenager is on his or her faith walk. She may have already said yes to Christ or she may be someone who doesn't even know what that means. Affirm wherever she is on her faith journey. You might even consider having him fill out a checklist at the beginning of your confirmation time together and see where he is. Then revisit this checklist at the end of your confirmation time to see how far your confirmand has grown. A resource checklist for you to use is at the end of this guide titled "My Life With Christ."

Teenagers are more likely to be engaged if they feel you care about them inside and *outside* the church setting.

- Teenagers are more likely to be engaged if they feel you care about them inside and *outside* the church setting. Start each meeting time with life questions like, "What is good in your life right now?" or "How was that soccer game or play you were in?" Get to know your teens and who they are. In reverse, while taking time for "life talk" is important, make sure it does not sidetrack you from the planned topic. Mentors report that during their time together, it's often hard to get the conversation back on track once it has derailed. Setting a time limit on "talking life" might be helpful for both of you when it's time to switch gears.

- During discussions make sure the words you use and your responses are helpful and supportive and create an environment where your teen feels safe to share any thoughts or feelings they might have. Young people will not contribute to a discussion if they are afraid they will be ridiculed when they talk. You can help create a sharing environment by the statements you make and feedback you give when your teen shares. Just simply saying something like, "I appreciate that thought" will encourage a young person to continue. Be mindful also of your body language when the teen shares. Leaning in, looking into the face, and nodding your head while the teen is talking show you are interested and actively listening to the person.

- While this may seem obvious, it does take practice to avoid yes/no questions with your teenager. Instead, ask "what," "why," or "how" questions that will lead to discussion. When a teen gives only short answers, ask the teen to elaborate by asking things like, "Why do you think that is?"

- Don't fear silence. This is one of the things talkers most struggle with when mentoring young people. You may be a talker. It's difficult but is critical. It can feel like an eternity when there is silence. But, in actuality, it can take a few minutes for a teen to formulate her or his thoughts into an answer to your question. There may be times when he or she simply has no response. There may be times when you may need to restate the question or thought, use a different example, split it apart, or throw out a "what if." But the important thing is to learn to hold your tongue and wait for your teen to respond.

- There are times when it is a good idea to hand out questions or thoughts in advance to give a young person time to think. Alternatively, if some thoughts or questions could use more time to develop, table them for the next time. Some teens might like time to write down thoughts before you discuss further.

- Make sure to leave time for any "other" questions they might have. And know they *will* have them. Questions are one of the greatest fears mentors have. "What if they ask something that I don't know the answer to?" Let's just say it's not if this will happen, but when. The fact that they are asking questions means they feel comfortable enough to do so. Take this as a compliment! If they ask a question you don't know the answer to, be honest with them. Acknowledge the question and rephrase it, making sure you understand what the teen really wants to know. If you need time to think on your answer, then simply let him or her know that you will look into it and get back with the teen on the best answer next time you meet.

- As you look into the questions, start with prayer asking the Holy Spirit to guide you. Then look at the Scriptures. What do the Scriptures say about the question or topic? What other resources are there that might help you point your confirmand in the right direction? Finally, use your own experience surrounding the question. Feel free to ask your youth minister or pastor to take a peek at your answer and see what they say about it as well. It's important to recognize that some questions can't be answered—only discussed and thought about. It's OK to not have all the answers. A chapter later in this guide will give you some direction on how to answer questions teens might have. The chapter also lists some of the top questions young people ask and thoughts on how to help the young person start to discover the answer.

- Show enthusiasm for the subject you're discussing. You can't expect teenagers to become interested in a discussion topic if you aren't. Do your homework on the topic you want to discuss, why it's interesting, worthwhile, and relevant. Do you have any personal experience with the topic? How does the topic relate to current events? Relating it to current events makes the connection between spiritual and the "real world." Feel free to bring in articles from newspapers or magazines or to show a YouTube video to tie the topic into young people's lives. This will help make the content relevant to your teen.

- Take time to pray for your confirmand and his or her family. Share joys and concerns with church staff as appropriate. You can simply ask your teen and/or his or her family if they would like pastoral prayer and support. Make sure and follow up joys and concerns from previous weeks. During your time together, make time to pray together over their joys and concerns. You may want to consider writing them down in a prayer journal or notebook so you can both see how God has been working over the weeks together. When your teen shares a concern with you, make sure to follow up during the week if it is something in need of prayer. If the young person has a play audition or tryout for a sports team, a simple text or e-mail saying you are thinking of your teen goes a long way. By doing this, you are again connecting your teen's life with his or her faith.

• Your confirmand wants to know you and spend time with you. Getting to know each other better is part of developing your relationship, and it takes time.

Your confirmand wants to know you and spend time with you.

So consider doing activities together that promote interaction and don't force you to hurry. Some ideas might be to attend a church service together, do a prayer walk around your church, volunteer together in the church, or do mission work in your community. There is no better way to grow a relationship than to serve alongside each other. This age group feels Jesus most when they are serving others. When our young people fill out evaluations at the end of the confirmation time, their No. 1 thing they enjoyed doing with their mentors and small group was mission work. In fact, they ask if we could have more opportunities to serve others during confirmation.

• We often get so involved with the details and scheduling that we forget to invoke the Holy Spirit—ask to be led as you mentor your teen. Ask the Holy Spirit to penetrate the heart and mind of your teen. Spending a few minutes before your time with them just praying silently to yourself will center you and get you ready for what's ahead.

• All mentors mentor differently; the most important thing is to be yourself! Teens will learn more from you if they can get to know the real you, so be genuine. Use real-life examples from your life when teaching a point. Your teen will learn from your stories, and this will create an authentic and real atmosphere. You may be worried that your teen isn't going to like hanging out with you, but I'm here to say that your teen will *love* getting to know you! Teens can never have too many caring adults in their lives.

Mentoring More Than One!

At the Church of the Resurrection, our mentors mentor a small group of young people with two or three mentors per group. My mentors are told up front that they are a mentoring team and should share responsibilities and work together. Each mentor can bring a particular gift to the relationship. While there are advantages to mentoring one young person at time, there are also advantages to being a part of a mentoring group.

- A mentor in a group situation doesn't feel alone on the confirmation journey and can use other mentors to bounce ideas off of or discuss situations with a particular young person. Many of my mentors sign up to partner with people they enjoy serving with or who have mentored them in their Christian walk. Mentoring with someone you know can make it fun.

- With the group mentoring approach, a new mentor is more likely to volunteer since he or she knows going into it that he or she will not be alone. I oftentimes will put an experienced mentor with one who is new so the new mentor can learn from the experienced one. The experienced mentors can share ideas that have worked for them in the past. They can also serve as encouragers when the new mentors may feel frustrated or unsure. Feeling encouraged and supported will often facilitate a new mentor choosing to serve as a confirmation mentor again.

- Many middle school confirmands who don't like to be the focus of attention like the group mentoring because they don't feel singled out or put on the spot. They can wait and hear what others in the group are saying during discussions and add their own thoughts as they are ready.

- In a mentoring team, each person on the team brings a unique gift. While some mentors are good at organizing and scheduling, others may be good at communication with parents and families. Some mentors might bring a unique way of teaching young people that is fun and creative. Each team can learn how to utilize their gifts to grow in relationship with their teens.

- If you have a mentor who moves, leaves the church, or experiences a major life change so that the mentor can no longer serve, there is a "backup" for young people to continue in relationship so that they don't have to begin again with a mentoring relationship. Consistency is key to the confirmands developing relationship. By having two or three mentors they are already connected with, then if one has to drop out of confirmation, the teen doesn't have to start over in building a relationship with a brand-new mentor.

- With a mentoring partner, you are not meeting with young people alone, which opens up more options of meeting places and spaces. You could meet in a classroom, for instance, whereas if you are alone, you need to meet in a public space.

- Lastly, it is nice to have another mentor hear what another mentor is saying. I have had parents call me before and say that their son or daughter came home and said that the teen's mentor said something a certain way. I am then able to not only go to the mentor to discuss it but also go to the co-mentor as well and see what was said and how it could have been interpreted by the teen a certain way. When we talk to teens, there are times when our words are not clear in a way they can understand. We don't want our confirmands to be left confused after a mentoring session.

It is up to each church and their ministry to decide what mentoring approach is best for their confirmation program and confirmands. Regardless of the choice, any kind of mentoring, whether it's one on one or shared mentoring, is an invaluable part of the confirmation student's faith journey.

Many former confirmation students tell me one of the main reasons they come on Sundays is to see their mentors. Knowing that someone cares and is looking out for them helps make faith real to young people. Whether in individual or group settings, mentoring creates the kind of Christian community where strong bonds are formed. And that's something we all seek.

Encouragement From Other Mentors

At the end of confirmation, I do a survey with my mentors to find out what we can do to improve their mentoring experience. To be honest, many of our confirmation program changes and ideas come from the minds and hearts of these amazing servants. So I thought it might be helpful for you to hear a few quotations and words of advice from mentors when I asked them, "What would you say to a person who is consider mentoring?"

- "Relax and have fun with the kids! Often times the best conversation comes from just letting them start talking about a topic rather than strictly following the curriculum to the letter. The more you let the kids make decisions and lead discussion, the more they listen, share, and ask questions."

  — Vicki

- "Every student will be on a different faith journey. Don't expect them to 'want' to be there at first. You will be blessed."

  — Ann

- "Just get to know them and spend more time with their personal things instead of only focusing on the curriculum. Great experience! I am so blessed to have been a part of it! I loved it so much more than I thought I would! Confirmation helped me grow in my own faith."

  — Siciley

- "Listen more than you talk. If you don't know the answer to one of their questions, tell them you'll let them know next week."

  —Brooke

- "Lighten up. Be authentic."

  —Shawn

- "Be flexible. Go where they lead you. It's about them and their experience, not you."

  —Raelene

- "Prepare and plan well in advance. Be very patient as these kids are at one of the toughest stages of their lives."

  —Dan

- "Don't be awkward working with the kids. . . . They won't approach you and ask meaningful questions or tell you what they're struggling with unless you're approachable. They'll love having someone that isn't their age talk to them. Don't be nervous."

  —Carter (one of our junior mentors)

- "Embrace the spiritual journey; be open to sharing your story and faith with them. I was so blessed to be a mentor! It was an incredible journey that I will never forget. I feel so much closer to God/Jesus because of it. Thank you!"

  —Beth

Hopefully the encouragement from these mentors will be of help to you in your relationship with your young person. Many of our mentors decide to mentor specifically because someone who has done it before says things like what you just read. I encourage you to share how amazing your experience was with others in your church so that the confirmation ministry will continue to grow.

5 Connecting With 'Confirm'

Your confirmand will be learning things each week as they go through the *Confirm* curriculum. As the confirmands are learning, it's important that you know what they are studying so you can support them in the process. The curriculum is divided into six units with each unit having a specific focus and theme. Below you will find a summary of each unit, an activity or icebreaker to go with it, and a few general starter questions as well as suggestions for ways they can take what they are learning into their church, home, and community relationships.

As the confirmands are learning, it's important that you know what they are studying so you can support them in the process.

Unit 1: Our Journey

1. Traveling Together

2. Living Together

3. Loving Together

4. Belonging Together

The confirmation journey is about equipping teens with the information, tools, and experiences they need to make an informed decision about committing to follow Christ. The first step in that journey is helping teens to understand the facets of Christian community. Not only will they learn how The United Methodist Church works, but they also will be given the chance to build meaningful and powerful relationships with one another, members of their family, and members of their church family. To that end, the first session of this journey is establishing the foundation for meaningful relationships between the teens and their guides for the journey, namely their teachers and mentors. The subsequent two sessions will explore the importance of belonging and participation in the Christian community and challenge the teens to start practicing what it means to live in Christian community. The final session will connect teens with a biblical understanding of belonging. Each step of the way, teens will be challenged to think more deeply about their faith, both personally and communally.

Icebreaker

Activity: "Would You Rather?"

Say: *"Over the next few weeks we are going to be learning about each other and developing our relationship, so let's play a game of 'Would You Rather?' to learn more about each other in a fun way."*

Mentors: Ask your confirmand a few of the following questions and then let your confirmand ask you a few. After each one, take time to ask some follow-up questions as to why the confirmand made the choice he or she did.

Ask: Would you rather

- Be good at sports or get good grades?

- Be able to fly or be able to breathe underwater?

- Get up early or stay up late?

- Drink a gallon of mustard or a gallon of ketchup?

- Be the smartest kid in school or the most popular kid in school?

- Not be able to shower or bathe for one month or not be able to brush your teeth for six months?

- Be a vegetarian or eat meat all day?

- Know your own future or know the future of your friends and not be able to tell them?

- Eat ten live earthworms or lie perfectly still for one hour in a box filled with them?

- Go forward or back in time?

- Be the most popular kid in school for five years or have one great friend forever?

- Eat five rotten cheese slices or eat a live cricket?

- Never be able to speak again or always have to say everything that is on your mind?

- Eat ice cream or have French fries?

- Be super fast or super strong?

- Be invisible or have the ability to fly?

- Have a third eye or a third arm?

- Be poor and work at a job you love or rich and work at a job you hate?

- Go without Internet or your phone for a month?

Conversation Starters

- Why are you going through confirmation?

- What are your thoughts on church?

- How would you describe a Christian?

Next Steps

- When you get home, ask your family who first introduced church to them. What are each family member's thoughts about church?

- If you are not already connected in church in some way, research two ways you might want to get involved and let your mentor know what you might be interested in.

- Find a way to show love to someone this week who might not be showing love to you. Share with your mentor your experience and how it made you feel. Was it difficult?

Unit 2: Our History and Heritage

1. The Faith of Jesus

2. The Early Church

3. The Reformation

4. Wesley and the Methodists

5. The Growth of Methodism

6. The Local Church

In order to truly understand our lives and beliefs, we must understand the lives and beliefs of the people who came before us. Our identity and faith are rooted in and shaped by the experiences of our spiritual ancestors traced back over the centuries.

These six lessons are designed to help you consider where your faith comes from in the hope that it will give you a better understanding of where it may be going. You'll be introduced to a long and diverse tradition that you're already a part of and encouraged to imagine how you might carry that tradition into the future.

Icebreaker

Activity: "Fact or Fiction."

Say: *"Since you are talking in this unit about the history of Christianity and the faith of Jesus, let's play a little game called 'Fact or Fiction.' I have a package of Skittles* (or any other candy with pieces) *here and I am going to read you a statement about Christianity. You decide if you think it is a fact or fiction. If you are correct, you get the piece of candy. If not, then I get the piece. Ready? Let's start!"*

Ask: Fact or fiction?

1. Followers of the Christian religion base their beliefs on the life, teachings, and death of Jesus Christ.
   (FACT.)

2. Christians believe many Gods created heaven, Earth, and the universe.
   (FICTION. Christians believe in one God that created heaven, Earth, and the universe.)

3. Christians believe Jesus Christ is the "Messiah" or Savior of the world.
   (FACT.)

4. Jesus' earthly father was a religious leader.
   (FICTION. He was carpenter; see Matthew 13:55.)

5. Many prophets predicted the coming of Christ, as written in multiple books of the Old Testament, according to Christian belief.
   (FACT.)

6. Jesus was born in a manger in Bethesda.
   (FICTION. Jesus was born in Bethlehem.)

7. Jesus was stoned to death.
   (FICTION. Jesus was crucified on a cross. His death made salvation and forgiveness of sins possible for all.)

8. The Bible is on the best-seller list.
   (FACT.)

9. Interpretations of the Bible and the practices of each church vary by denomination, but the belief in one God and Jesus as the Messiah is central to all Christians.
   (FACT.)

10. The name *Jesus* translates to mean "redeemer."
    (FICTION. The name *Jesus* means "Savior." It is the same name as Joshua in the Old Testament.)

11. During the sixth century, it was customary to congratulate people who sneezed because it was thought that they were expelling evil from their bodies. During the great plague of Europe, the Pope passed a law to say "God bless you" to one who sneezed.
    (FACT.)

12. There are thirty-five books in the Bible: ten in the Old Testament, twenty-five in the New Testament.
    (FICTION. There are sixty-six books in the Bible: thirty-nine in the Old Testament, twenty-seven in the New Testament.)

13. The word "Christian" appears only three times in the Bible: Acts 11:26; Acts 26:28; and 1 Peter 4:16.
    (FACT.)

14. Christianity is not the world's largest religion.
    (FICTION. Christianity is the world's largest religion with approximately 2.1 billion Christians.)

What values should a Christian have that are most important to you?

Conversation Starters

1. What do you know about your own family history?

2. What does being a Christian mean to you?

3. What values should a Christian have that are most important to you?

Next Steps

1. Ask your parents what they know about the history of their own families. Ask your family to help you draw a family tree listing your siblings, parents, aunts and uncles, grandparents, and great-grandparents. Go back as far as you want or you are able. Share this with your mentor next time you meet.

2. Spend some time researching about your own church.

   a. When/where was it started?

   b. What conference is it in?

   c. How many members do you have?

   d. What is your church's purpose and/or mission statement?

Unit 3: Our Life Together

1. The Connection

2. Simple Worship

3. Music and Lyrics

4. Remembrance

5. Accepting Grace

6. A Loving Church

7. So Now What?

In Our Life Together, your group will jump with both feet into much of what makes the practice of United Methodism unique among other Protestant denominations. We'll explore everything from how our church is organized to how we worship together! Young people will learn about the instrumental role our hymnal plays in preparing for worship, as well as what we believe about our practices of Holy Communion and baptism. The unit then provides an introduction to the United Methodist Social Principles, our guide to how to be United Methodists in our world. We close with a reminder that our understanding of social issues is meaningless unless we also take action on what we believe together! Your group will emerge from Our Life Together with not only a better understanding of our global church but also a better understanding of what it means to be confirmed.

Icebreaker

Activity: "Who Am I?"

Say: *"Since you have been talking about who you are as a Christian and who we are as Methodists, let's play a game called 'Who Am I?'"*

Mentors: Pick one of you to be the Mystery Person first and the other to be the Guesser. Whoever is the Mystery Person thinks of a person, living or dead. The Guesser gets ten yes or no questions to ask the Mystery Person to see if the Guesser can figure out the identity. Once the round is over, switch roles and let the new Mystery Person pick a person, living or dead.

Conversation Starters

- Who sets the rules in your house? What are some rules you have?

- What part of worship really speaks to you?

- What does taking Communion mean to you?

- What social things going on in the world right now do you wish you could be more involved in?

Next Steps

- Find at least one way you can be involved in leadership in your church, school, and community. Report back to your mentor what ways in each you might be interested in.

- Meet with your pastor or youth minister and give two ways you feel they can encourage and include youth leadership in the church.

- Scroll though the *USA TODAY* website or app on your phone. What social issues going on right now do you feel Christians could have a positive impact on? Share your thoughts with a friend or family member.

Unit 4: Our Beliefs

1. Faith and Trust

2. Experiencing God

3. The Bible: Not Just a History Book

4. The Bible: A Methodist's View

5. The Holy Trinity

6. Who Is God? (And Who God Isn't)

7. Praying: Talking with God

8. Prayer: Listening to God

Believing in something is taking a step toward the unknown and having the humility to realize that mystery will always be present. It is our human condition to want to know everything, but when we know something, there is left no

Trusting is an important part of our faith as Christians. Not only do we need to trust others, but we need to trust in our God as well.

room for belief. God wants us to believe. The beauty of our relationship with our Creator is that we don't know everything yet we can trust God—we can trust God to be a part of our lives in ways that we do not understand. And when we truly trust in God, we can then respond in ways that transform the world toward the possibilities of God's kingdom.

What we believe is important—both communally and individually. The United Methodist Church has doctrine that states her institutional beliefs, but she also acknowledges that we are individuals with unique perspectives. Belief is not about being "right" but rather about providing a structure to create a communal identity and a skeletal framework for individual belief. As we take a journey with God, we discover how our church can form our beliefs but also how we individually process our understanding of God.

Icebreaker

Activity: "Trust Draw."

Say: *"Trusting is an important part of our faith as Christians. Not only do we need to trust others, but we need to trust in our God as well. Since we are growing in our relationship together, I want you to be able to trust me as well. So we are going to do a trust drawing activity. I am thinking of an object in my head and I'm going to blindfold you* (or ask them to close their eyes) *and give you a blank piece of paper. I want you to trust that I can get you to draw what I am thinking in my head. I will give you directions. Let's see how well we can do trusting each other."*

Mentors: For instance, if you want to have your teen draw a picture of a car, say, *"Draw a rectangle. Now draw four small circles under your rectangle,"* and so on. Other things you can choose for drawing could be a smiley face, a house, a dog, an airplane, and so on. If time allows, you can switch roles.

Conversation Starters

- Let's read James 2:14-20 from our Bibles or on our phones. What does James say faith is? What does having faith mean to you?

- Can you have trust in God but still question God?

- How does the Trinity (Father, Son, and Holy Spirit) help you to understand who God is?

Next Steps

- Make a list of those you can trust in your life.

- Faith is not just about belief, but it's also about action. Find one way to act on your faith this week at school or in the community. Was it hard or easy to do?

- Pick one of your favorite Bible verses this week. (Mentors, share one of yours for an example.) Read the verse and write down what it means to you. Next, read the chapter it's in. Does it change the meaning for you? Now read the chapters before and after the one you just read. Did reading the context of the verse make a difference in its original meaning to you?

Unit 5: Our Theology

1. Looking Like God: The Imago Dei

2. Hitting the Mark: Sin and Grace

3. Two Natures, One Man: Who is Jesus?

4. What is Salvation?

5. Divine Helper: The Holy Spirit as Guide

6. What's Next: Life After Death

7. From Whence We Came: The Creeds

What we believe as Christians, or our theology, is the foundational truths that empower us to understand the Christian faith with both our hearts and minds. This holistic understanding of our theology empowers us to share the principles of our faith in meaningful, purposeful ways. Over the next seven lessons, you will confirm what you may already know about Jesus, the Holy Spirit, and salvation and uncover new ways of understanding Christian thoughts around sin and grace and the rich legacy that a life with Christ leaves for others to follow into eternity.

Icebreaker

Activity: Molding clay.

Say: *"Since we are made in the image of God, I want you to take the time to think about what God's image looks like to you. I brought some clay and I want us to each spend some time molding it into your 'image' of God."*

Mentors: Do this activity along with your teen. Take time when you are done to share your moldings and discuss them.

Conversation Starters

- What is a sin to you? How does it make you feel to know that you are forgiven for your sins?

- What reason do you think Jesus had for also being fully human when he came to be with us?

- Have you ever felt the Holy Spirit "nudge" you to do something or say something? What was it? Did you listen?

Next Steps

- Ask everyone in your family to draw a picture of who God is to them. Share with each other why you each drew what you did.

- Ask the Holy Spirit to guide you to help someone in need this week. It could be as simple as inviting a fellow student to join you at the lunch table or over to your home. Maybe it's helping a neighbor or family member in need of assistance.

- Read the Apostles' Creed. Think about how each part of the creed reflects a part of our beliefs as Christians. Are parts of this creed easier for you to believe? Are there some that you struggle with? Share these thoughts with your mentor next time you meet.

Unit 6: Our Faith and Calling

1. A Faith to Decide

2. A Faith to Confirm

3. A Faith to Live

4. A Call to Follow

5. A Spirit to Find

6. A Story to Tell

7. A Journey to Continue

Our faith and the living out of our faith, also known as our calling, are intricately linked. James 2:17 says, "In the same way, faith is dead when it doesn't result in faithful activity." When we live our faith, our calling is clarified and our relationship with God is strengthened. As our encounters with God clarify who we are, our faith becomes even deeper. We cannot fully understand either faith or calling without the other. This unit will challenge teens to put together all they have been learning over the past sessions and articulate what they believe in their own words. They will be pushed to take seriously their faith and discipleship through realistic examination of the United Methodist baptismal vows and the living out of those vows within the life of their congregation.

Ultimately, each teen will have to decide for himself or herself if being confirmed in The United Methodist Church is a calling he or she is willing and able to accept.

Icebreaker

Activity: Rock, Paper, Scissors.

Say: *"As you are coming to the end of your confirmation journey, you will be making the decision as to whether you want to be confirmed or not. So let's play a quick game of Rock, Paper, Scissors to see how you are on your decision-making abilities."*

Mentors: Play the best three out of five rounds before declaring a winner.

Conversation Starters

- How do you make decisions?

- What questions do you still have before you get confirmed?

- How have you grown in confirmation?

Next Steps

- Spend time writing a letter to God telling God how you feel about your upcoming confirmation and what your next steps will be to continue on this journey. Ask your mentor or your parent to keep the letter and mail it to you one month after confirmation is over.

- Write a thank you note to your mentor. Share with your mentor how he or she has impacted your faith.

- Think of family members, friends, or other adults who have supported and encouraged you on your confirmation journey. Send a quick text telling them.

6 Continuing the Conversation After Confirmation

Despite our desire and commitment for lasting relationships, one of the most difficult things as a mentor you might encounter is not seeing your confirmand engaged in the life of the church after he or she is confirmed. While it doesn't address confirmation per se, a Barna study indicates that "40 percent to 50 percent of all youth group graduates fail to stick with their faith or connect with a faith community after high school."[1] When you spend time with a young person and her or his family investing in the young person with your heart and soul, this is not just a high statistic but a face and a friend. Getting confirmed is the easy part; staying connected and on the faith journey is the hard part.

Getting confirmed is the easy part; staying connected and on the faith journey is the hard part.

As adults, we understand how staying connected with our church community takes effort and commitment, especially when life is hard. For teens, it takes relationships. A Fuller Youth Institute study reports that "churches and families wanting to instill deep faith in youth should help them build a web of relationships with committed and caring adults."[2] In his book *Sustainable Youth Ministry,* Mark DeVries shares that "4–6 is the amount of teenagers that an adult can know intimately in a spiritual mentor type role."[3]

This is why you as a mentor are so important. As confirmation leaders, we see new young people each year, but as a mentor you have the opportunity to know one or more of them intimately in a way that the confirmation director or pastor cannot. When you do, you give your teens their best opportunity for a long life of following Jesus.

What's Next?

Most confirmation programs have a defined period of time and expectations, but when it's over, a confirmand might wonder, "What comes next?" As a mentor, you will make the difference by preparing your student for their next steps. Rather than wait until the last weeks of the confirmation process, it's important that this preparation starts from the very beginning. Let them know that what they do in confirmation is not just a checklist, but rather practices that need to continue beyond to grow in Christ. With every new learning, help them imagine how they will live as followers of Jesus outside and beyond the class. Take time each mentoring session to remind them that participating in the life of the church, prayer, and other spiritual disciplines will need to continue for them to continue to grow.

Get Them Connected

As mentioned earlier, a key to keeping your teenager involved after confirmation is to make sure they are connected in the life of the church. We know teenagers and families are busy and over-scheduled. Making sure your teen has a weekly connection with a part of the church is critical when confirmation is over. Tell young people that getting involved in the church is not about making them busier, but inviting them to be part of a family that will miss them when they haven't been around in some time. We want them to be missed! As a mentor, it's part of your responsibility to help your confirmand find his or her place where he or she can volunteer and serve in the life of your church.

This connection needs to be made early in the confirmation process. Some areas you can connect them in your church might include the nursery, children's programming, ushering, greeting, the technology team, working in the office, participating in youth group or choir, or serving on a church board or ministry team. Every church can use these amazing young people in some way. Teens are not the future of the church but with us, the church today. If they are not already serving in a ministry area, you can facilitate a connection for them by:

1. Learning what his or her interests are.

2. Setting up a meeting with a leader in that ministry area and your confirmand. You may offer to attend the meeting with them.

No one knows these young people better than their mentors. Once they are connected, you can both encourage them and hold them accountable for fulfilling their commitment to serve by having them share about their experiences when you meet. When you do this, you are inviting others in their church community to know and love your confirmand and be another in the cloud of witnesses in her or his faith journey.

No one knows these young people better than their mentors.

Spiritual Practices

Spiritual practices (or disciplines) are means of grace by which we can grow closer to Jesus. Spiritual practices include prayer, Bible study, worship, service, and others.[4] Since each young person is unique, you may want to explore with your teen which spiritual disciplines or practices he or she is naturally inclined toward and which ones he or she may need direction on. Practice them together in your mentoring meetings and encouraging your teen to practice the ones he or she struggles with on his or her own, as it takes practice to create a consistent rhythm. Let your confirmand know that it's OK that it feels awkward at first and that even as adults we continue to work on spiritual practices.

Parents As Partners

In the article "Helping Kids Keep The Faith," Dustin McClure says that "parents continue to be the single greatest influence on their children's faith."[5] Your confirmand's family will be around and involved in his or her life long after confirmation is over. Part of the job of the church is to support, encourage, and nurture the family to fulfill their responsibility to nurture their teen's faith. Here are some ways you can help enhance this relationship:

- Develop a relationship with the parents from the beginning of confirmation, asking them to share with you ways you can help their child in his or her confirmation journey.

- Encourage communication with the parents, sending them updates on their son's or daughter's progress. Let them know they can contact you as well with questions coming up at home that you can help address in mentoring sessions.

- Ask them to let you know when things come up in their family or teen's life that you might be able to support them in. This can be through prayer or pastoral support or resources the church might have.

- Before confirmation is over, let them know what you and their son or daughter have discussed as ways to continue in the life of the church, whether that is mission work, volunteering in a ministry area, or simply attending weekly service together.

A few years ago, a confirmand turned in a handwritten prayer card to our prayer ministry asking for our pastors to pray for her family to come to church regularly again like they did during confirmation. This prayer card is heartbreaking, but it does help to remind us that our job is not only to ensure that confirmands understand that the church is the place for a lifelong faith journey but also to help their families realize it as well.

Stay the Course

Make sure you are attending to your spiritual life and important relationships.

As a mentor, you have one of the most important roles in the confirmation program. Therefore, it is vital that you stay the course. Giving so much time, energy, and effort to a young person can be draining. Make sure you are attending to your spiritual life and important relationships. Tough issues, questions, and situations will come up. Find out early where to go for help so that you will feel equipped, encouraged, and supported as a mentor.

You are not alone in this process. Mentors also need mentoring at times.

You are not alone in this process. Mentors also need mentoring at times. Your mentoring can come from a variety of places. Ask for support and guidance through prayers from those in your church community. Your confirmation leader may connect you with more "experienced" mentors in a more formal training process. If not, seek out your children's director, youth director, or pastor for support. Any of these people are there to talk with, share ideas and resources with, and provide inspiration and encouragement to help you be the best mentor you can be.

You were called and equipped by the Holy Spirit to be a mentor as it says in 1 Corinthians 12:4-7 (ESV):

> Now there are varieties of gifts, but the same Spirit; and there are varieties of service, but the same Lord; and there are varieties of activities, but it is the same God who empowers them all in everyone. To each is given the manifestation of the Spirit for the common good.

Even though there are times you might feel like you are not doing all you can for your confirmand, never doubt the impact you have. Proverbs 22:6 says, "Train children in the way they should go; when they grow old, they won't depart

Your confirmands are writing the early chapters of their faith stories together with God, their families, you, and your congregation.

from it." You are planting seeds. All the seeds you plant now may not grow or mature now, but with a little "watering" from the Holy Spirit, they WILL grow. Just keep on planting.

Your confirmands are writing the early chapters of their faith stories together with God, their families, you, and your congregation. I trust that when you help them get connected with their faith community, help them incorporate spiritual practices in their lives, partner with parents, and commit to stay the course, your confirmands will begin to realize what God has in store for them now and beyond confirmation.

Chapter 6 Notes

1. "What Makes Faith Stick During College?," PRWeb website, 13 September 2011, *tinyurl.com/h89qb4w*. Accessed 15 September 2016. The article references previous studies: Barna Update, "Most Twentysomethings Put Christianity on the Shelf Following Spiritually Active Teen Years," The Barna Group, 2006, 16 September 2006; George H. Gallup, Jr., The Gallup Poll, 2006; and Christian Smith with Patricial Snell, *Souls in Transition* (New York: Oxford University Press, 2009), pages 105, 108, 109, and 116.
2. "What Makes Faith Stick During College?"
3. "7 Youth Ministry Numbers You Really Should Know," by Gavin Richardson, 4 October 2011, Youthworker Movement website *tinyurl.com/jm6e6sc*. Accessed 14 September 2016.
4. For a full list of spiritual practices, read "The Wesleyan Means of Grace," The United Methodist Church website, *umc.org/how-we-serve/the-wesleyan-means-of-grace*. Accessed 12 October 2016.
5. "Helping Kids Keep the Faith," by Dustin McClure, 15 December 2013, Fuller Youth Institute website, *fulleryouthinstitute.org/articles/helping-kids-keep-the-faith*. Accessed 10 October 2016.

7 Those Questions!

Guidance From John Wesley

As a mentor you will field questions from your confirmands. Scripture tells us that Jesus was about your confirmand's age when He stayed to discuss questions in the temple (Luke 2:41-52). So it's natural that your young people will be wanting to talk about faith questions at their age. While this might be a challenge, mentors report that when they answer their confirmands' questions, they themselves learn. As was discussed earlier, some questions cannot be answered fully and you may not know the answer, but it's important for you as a mentor to give opportunity for each question to be heard and discussed. And remember, it is OK to leave questions unanswered. Often the tension of an unanswered question promotes further inquiry and discovery.

Creating an open, safe, and healthy environment for honest questions will be an important priority. John Wesley, the founder of the Methodist movement, followed this approach: Unity in the essentials, in the non-essentials liberty. In all things charity.[1] Valuing unity reminds us that as followers of Christ we are one body, one church, "the communion of saints," as said in the Apostles' Creed.[2] Unity should characterize how we approach disagreements in any discussion on spiritual things.

Remembering this approach can serve as a guide on how to approach questions that young people are raising in their faith. Here's how:

- There will be questions about what we consider "essential" or "core" to our faith and theology (for example, Jesus the Son of God, God the Creator) that are taught in confirmation. To be confirmed, each confirmand will have to commit to believing the essentials. The mentor role is not to convince but rather gently persuade and respond to their questions that reflect the journey of discovering the truth they are on. There will be young people in your group who are far from the point of making a faith commitment. Continue to mentor them in a gentle and kind way just as you would one who is saying yes to Jesus.

- There will be discussions on what are considered "non-essentials." These are teachings that are not core to our faith, that do not affect the ability of a young person to be confirmed, and where there can be disagreement and yet unity. Examples include the Creation story, the end times, and signs and wonders. When discussing teenagers' questions, never allow a non-essential issue to become essential.

When discussing teenagers' questions, never allow a non-essential issue to move into the essentials.

- Respecting our differences is where "in all things charity" comes in. Promote respect for each person and each person's freedom to share her or his perspective.

- Finally, many of their questions will be difficult to answer and will only be answered by the teenagers discovering the answers themselves.

Let Romans 15:5-7 also guide you:

May the God of endurance and encouragement give you the same attitude toward each other, similar to Christ Jesus' attitude. That way you can glorify the God and Father of our Lord Jesus Christ together with one voice. So welcome each other, in the same way that Christ also welcomed you, for God's glory.

A Guide for Discussions

One way you can help confirmands discover the answers
to their questions is to use what is called the Wesleyan
Quadrilateral. It consists of:

- **Scripture**—The Bible. John Wesley considered
  Scripture to be foundational and the primary source
  and criterion for Christian doctrine and life. As
  United Methodists, the starting point is always the
  Scripture; we use the other three things to help
  us understand and interpret the Scripture. When
  looking at a question, research what the Bible says in
  reference to it.

- **Tradition**—Our heritage and faith. What have
  Christians done and believed through the ages?
  Looking back on what we have believed and
  practiced in the past will help put a frame of
  reference on the questions the confirmands are
  asking today.

- **Experience**—What is true in our own lives, our faith,
  and our experiences with God? How do your own
  personal experiences and encounters surrounding
  the question impact it? What does Scripture have
  to say about our experiences? Remember there is
  much we haven't experienced and still much to learn,
  so we should be willing to learn from others' life
  experiences and lives of faith as well.

- **Reason**—This is our God-given ability to think
  through faith issues rationally in order to come to a
  sensible faith commitment.

Reflection: Using these four lenses and relying on the Holy
Spirit will help to guide us. God wants us to discover our faith
and God's truths, not simply to be told by others what to believe.

Below are some of the most frequently asked questions
your confirmands may have. The information following each

question should serve as a guide, a resource for you as you approach them. Guided by the Quadrilateral approach, both you and your confirmand should research what Scripture says, what tradition has said around this question, and how your own experiences and ability to reason can impact how you look at this question. Finally, encourage confirmands to use their reason to take all of these and discern what they believe about the question for themselves.

How can I have a personal relationship with God?

How do you get to know your friends? You hang out with them. You spend time with them. That's the same with God. Confirmation is a good start, but you need to find ways to stay connected with other Christians on your faith journey—attending church, youth group, or Sunday School are examples. Christian fellowship is a great way to spend time with God because you're all of the same mindset and can also hold each other accountable.

Some ways you can deepen your relationship with God:

- **Pray.** Even if it's short, if it's sincere, God will listen and answer.

- **Read the Bible.** The Bible is God's love story God wrote for us. It has direction, guidance, and support for us in its words.

- **Memorize Scripture.** Don't memorize it just to memorize it. Memorize it so you know its meaning and you can apply it to your life. There will be situations in your life when God's Word can strengthen, encourage, and direct you when you most need it.

- **Don't quench the Holy Spirit's work within you.** Take time to listen to the "nudges" the Holy Spirit places in your heart. Maybe it will be changing a direction you were going, or calling or reaching out to a friend.

- **Journaling.** Spending quiet time reflecting on Scriptures you have read or just quieting your mind will enable God to speak through your thoughts. Writing these thoughts down will help you look back later at how God spoke to you.

- **Keep your actions and choices reflective of who you are striving to be as a Christian.** Think about "pruning" things in your life that draw you away from God.

The more you know about God, the more you'll love God. The more you love God, the more you'll want to obey God!

> *"You must love the Lord your God with all your heart, with all your being, with all your strength, and with all your mind, and love your neighbor as yourself."* (Luke 10:27)

Where did God come from?

God was not created; God has always existed. This is impossible for us to understand because everything else we know about has a beginning and an end (finite). But God has no beginning and God has no end (infinite). God always was, and God always will be. It's hard for us to understand how this could be possible. Beginnings and endings are limitations of our world but not of God. That is one of the great things about God. God is so much greater than we are! John 1:1-3 says:

> In the beginning was the Word and the Word was with God and the Word was God. The Word was with God in the beginning. Everything came into being through the Word, and without the Word nothing came into being.

How do you know when God forgives you?

We are born broken and sinful in a broken and sinful world. The more we let the Holy Spirit lead us in our lives and have control, the more we'll want to do more of what God wants us to do versus what WE want to do. That's why we have to continue to confess and repent. We might not experience an overwhelming relief and sense of God's love when we're forgiven. This is when trusted friends, mentors, and the Scriptures can help remind us that God loves us even when we feel unlovable and forgiven when we feel unforgivable. There will be many moments though when we will feel the love of God and God's forgiveness penetrate our hearts in small ways. One of John Wesley's most storied moments occurred when he sat and listened to an introduction to the book of Romans read at Aldersgate. Following the church meeting, he wrote: "I felt my heart strangely warmed. I felt I did trust in Christ, Christ alone for salvation, and an assurance was given me that he had taken away *my* sins, even *mine*, and saved *me* from the law of sin and death."[3]

What is the difference between God and the Holy Spirit?

The Holy Spirit is the third part of the Trinity—the Father, the Son (Jesus), and the Holy Spirit. To think of the Trinity in a simplistic way is really hard to do. It's important to know that even the most brilliant scholars realize the Trinity has a component of mystery involved in understanding the relationship. "The Articles of Religion of the Methodist Church" explains it this way:

> There is but one living and true God, everlasting, without body or parts, of infinite power, wisdom, and goodness; the maker and preserver of all things, both visible and invisible. And in unity of this Godhead there are three persons, of one substance, power, and eternity—the Father, the Son, and the Holy Ghost.[4]

From *The Book of Discipline of The United Methodist Church—2012.* Copyright © 2012 by The United Methodist Publishing House. Used by permission. All rights reserved.

It might be helpful to think of the Trinity in terms of the classical language that has helped to sustain the Church's imagination about:

- God the Father is God for us.
- God the Son is Jesus, God with us.
- God the Holy Spirit is God in us.

When Jesus was on this earth, he could be in only one place at a time. He also knew when he died, we would need his guidance and direction. Therefore, he sent the Holy Spirit to dwell in us. In John 14:26, Jesus is speaking: "The Companion the Holy Spirit, whom the Father will send in my name, will teach you everything and will remind you of everything I told you." The Holy Spirit works in our lives to remind us of what Jesus taught and gives power to be God's witnesses.

> Rather, you will receive power when the Holy Spirit has come upon you, and you will be my witnesses in Jerusalem, in all Judea and Samaria, and to the end of the earth." (Acts 1:8)

How do you know God is listening to your prayers?

The word *omnipresent* is one of characteristics used to describe God. It means God is *always* present with you. So God is there, but it's up to you to believe that. That's when faith comes in. "Faith is the reality of what we hope for, the proof of what we don't see" (Hebrews 11:1). We can't see God face to face; however, God's presence is in us through the Holy Spirit. We pray, even though God already knows our prayers, to have a conversation with God. How well would you know anyone else if you never talked to them? Prayer is one way to get to know God. Being a Christian is *not* a one-way street. While God might not speak to you directly to answer your prayers (God *does* answer them—yes, no, wait), you will receive an answer.

In your heart *know* that God is always with you and then pray knowing God *is* listening and has an answer for all your prayers! Even Jesus prayed. Do you think Jesus would pray if he didn't think God was there for him?

Those Questions!

I've never heard God talk to me. Is there something wrong with me?

God speaks to everyone; the problem is that we are not always listening. Wouldn't it be great if you could just get a notification on your phone that God sent you a text message? That would be so much easier! Unfortunately, God doesn't communicate that way. God talks to us in other ways we just don't always recognize it. Here are some ways God talks to us:

- **Through others.** Have you ever had someone say something nice to you or suggest you do something? That may be God trying to tell you that you are amazing or God wants you to do something for someone else.

- **Reading Scripture.** You could read the same Scripture over and over and each time it could mean something different to you, or two people could read the same Scripture and get two different thoughts. That is God speaking to you through the Scriptures.

- **Quiet voice.** In a typical day how many electronic devices do you have coming at you at once? Television, computer, gaming system, or a phone. All these are great, but they don't let you hear God talking to you in the silence. God may be telling you at lunch at school to sit with someone who needs a friend, but you might be too busy and caught up in your own world to stop and listen.

- **Listening.** How often when you pray do you stop and just listen? Most of the time we do all the talking when we pray to God. It's important that we take the time to listen for God in the silence.

Look! I'm standing at the door and knocking. If any hear my voice and open the door, I will come in to be with them, and will have dinner with them, and they will have dinner with me. (Revelation 3:20)

Should I believe the Bible word for word? Is it OK to disagree with things in the Bible?

It's important to look back on the statement made earlier referencing that the non-essentials mean that as Christians we may look at some things that are not essentials to our faith differently than other Christians do. So, the real question is, Can we disagree with how we interpret the Bible? It is OK to question the non-essentials in the Bible. The people who wrote the Bible were like us. The biblical authors wrote in particular times, for particular audiences, out of a particular context. Part of understanding Scripture is reading it in the light of what we can know about the history and culture of that time, what the author was trying to say in writing, and to whom the author was writing.

United Methodists believe that the Bible is "the inspired Word of God." In Latin the word *inspire* means to "breathe into," meaning that we believe God "breathed into" the writings of the Bible. We believe that it not only reveals God, but shows God's will to us.

> Every scripture is inspired by God and is useful for teaching, for showing mistakes, for correcting, and for training character, (2 Timothy 3:16)

The Bible is God's self-revelation (through inspiration) through Scripture that guides us in life.

Did God create evil?

In God's goodness, God created humanity with free will. The free will we have offers people the ability to choose good (follow God) or evil. Sometimes people, individually and collectively, choose evil instead of good. People often wonder what the difference is between sin and evil. Evil is a system of thought and/or activity that opposes God (Zechariah 7:9-10, Psalm 34:14). Parts of the Christian church personify evil in the world by naming the devil as evil or the evil one (John 17:15). Sin is missing the mark. Sin is an action that goes against God's will.

Those Questions! 67

God's image just like me. Nothing can overcome the power and grace that God offers us all! Our job is to love others as Christ loves us.

Persons who are gay or lesbian are no less individuals of sacred worth than persons who are heterosexual. All persons need the ministry and guidance of the church in their struggles for human fulfillment, as well as the spiritual and emotional care of a fellowship that enables reconciling relationships with God, with others, and with self. According to *The United Methodist Church Book of Discipline,*

> We affirm that all persons are individuals of sacred worth, created in the image of God. All persons need the ministry of the Church in their struggles for human fulfillment, as well as the spiritual and emotional care of a fellowship that enables reconciling relationships with God, with others, and with self. The United Methodist Church does not condone the practice of homosexuality and considers this practice incompatible with Christian teaching. We affirm that God's grace is available to all. We will seek to live together in Christian community, welcoming, forgiving, and loving one another, as Christ has loved and accepted us. We implore families and churches not to reject or condemn lesbian and gay members and friends. We commit ourselves to be in ministry for and with all persons.[6]

It's important to point out at this time that some United Methodists do not agree with this statement found in *The Book of Discipline.*[7] The United Methodist Church is currently in a discernment process around issues of human sexuality in hopes of arriving at a decision that provides a way for the United Methodist denomination to move forward and to faithfully fulfill our mission to make disciples for the transformation of the world.[8]

70

Why do bad things happen to good people?

The bigger question is, "Why doesn't God prevent it from happening?" If God is really an all-good and all-powerful being, why doesn't God do something?

As mentioned earlier, God does not create evil; God allows it to occur for the time being. When God originally created the world, God created all things good. God created people, however, with free will—the freedom to choose. This includes the freedom to make right and wrong choices.

Of course, God could intervene and control everything about our lives—the good and the bad—but then we would merely be robots and not truly free. God could even force us to love God if God wanted, but then forced love isn't true love. God gives us the freedom to choose or not to choose God, the freedom to live and enjoy life, and the freedom to make right and wrong choices. Unfortunately, we are left to deal with the consequences of our own and other people's actions.

In life we will have trials and difficulties. God often uses the trials of life for a greater good, often to develop our character and make us better people. And we are able to help others in similar circumstances. Trials also force us to see what is important in life, and often drive us to God when nothing else will. We see the importance of faith, of love, of caring, and of family and friends.

God never promised life would be problem-free. Remember at the end of the Creation story, God saw creation and said it was good. God didn't say it was "perfect." God did promise to be with people. Jesus himself felt love, compassion, and sorrow, and was drawn like a magnet to those who were hurting. God, in God's love, wants a relationship with us.

> God so loved the world that he gave his only Son, so that everyone who believes in him won't perish but will have eternal life. (John 3:16)

Will my pet be in heaven?

God cares for all of God's creation. This care is shown in
Genesis as God formed all that is and called it good. This care
is also shown in the Book of Revelation when God makes all
things new. We see in Romans 8:21 that the Scripture says
"that the creation itself will be set free from slavery to decay
and brought into the glorious freedom of God's children."
God cares for creation. I can't say for sure, but my hope is
that my pets and I become part of God's new creation.

Are angels real?

According to the Bible, angels were created by God. The
word *angel* means "messenger." Angels are God's messengers.
Angels can also be protectors and defenders (Genesis 3:24,
Numbers 22:31, 1 Chronicles 21:16). In the Bible we read
about people who saw angels. Sometimes people knew
they were angels, and sometimes they did not. Some angels
described in the Bible have wings, but many appeared as
human beings when they came to deliver messages to people
in the Bible. Below are some Scriptures about angels:

> Each of the four living creatures had six wings, and
> each was covered all around and on the inside with
> eyes. They never rest day or night, but keep on saying,
> "Holy, holy, holy is the Lord God Almighty, who was
> and is and is coming." (Revelation 4:8)

> "Be careful that you don't look down on one of these
> little ones. I say to you that their angels in heaven are
> always looking into the face of my Father who is in
> heaven. (Matthew 18:10)

> Look, there was a great earthquake, for an angel from
> the Lord came down from heaven. Coming to the
> stone, he rolled it away and sat on it. (Matthew 28:2)

What does heaven look like?

Heaven is sometimes described as God's dwelling place (1 Kings 8:30)—a place or context where God's will is done. God dwells where God's will is done so heaven looks like God's will being done. The Bible also talks about resurrection and new creation in Revelation 21. The Bible uses some wonderful imagery to give us a sense of what new creation is. Scripture tells of streets made of gold that we will walk on in the new Jerusalem.

> The twelve gates were twelve pearls; each one of the gates was made from a single pearl. And the city's main street was pure gold, as transparent as glass.
> (Revelation 21:21)

The best way to picture new creation is to imagine every good thing in this world being made new—perfected in and created by God's will.

> "Behold the dwelling place of God is with man. He will dwell with them as he is God. He will wipe away every tear from their eyes and death shall be no more, neither shall there be mourning or crying or pain anymore for the former things have passed away."
> (Revelation 21:3-4)

How do science and the Bible fit together?

As Christians, we accept that God created human beings and largely everything else that exists on earth. There is an idea that if modern science conflicts with the Genesis account of Creation, modern science must be wrong, therefore forcing people to choose one or the other, between science and God. What if we approach the Creation story not as a science lesson? The Bible is a way for us to answer the who and why of Creation, not specifically the how and when. What if we look at the Genesis account in the Bible as an account of our beliefs and truths that God is good, creation is good, and life is a gift? Evolution doesn't diminish God's glory, meaning God created life, but evolution can be explained on how things change over time. God built it, evolution is how it changes and adapts over time. Can't science and the Bible teach truth?

> The heavens declare the glory of God, and the sky above proclaims his handiwork. (Psalm 19:1, ESV)

> In the beginning, God created the heavens and the earth. (Genesis 1:1, ESV)

Chapter 7 Notes

1. "Section 2: Our Doctrinal History," The United Methodist Church website, *umc. org/what-we-believe/section-2-our-doctrinal-history.* Accessed 10 October 2016.
2. "Apostles' Creed: Traditional and Ecumenical Versions," The United Methodist Church website, *umc.org/what-we-believe/apostles-creed-traditional-ecumenical.* Accessed 10 October 2016.
3. From *The Works of John Wesley, Volume 18,* eds. W. Reginald Ward and Richard P. Heitzenrater (Nashville: Abingdon Press, 1988), page 250.
4. From *The Book of Discipline of The United Methodist Church—2012.* Copyright © 2012 by The United Methodist Publishing House; ¶ 104, pages 63-64. Used by permission. All rights reserved.
5. From *The Book of Discipline of The United Methodist Church—2012.* Copyright © 2012 by The United Methodist Publishing House; ¶ 162B, page 117. Used by permission. All rights reserved.
6. From *The Book of Discipline of The United Methodist Church—2012.* Copyright © 2012 by The United Methodist Publishing House; ¶ 161F, page 111. Used by permission. All rights reserved.
7. "Poll: Small Changes in Church Homosexuality Views," by Heather Hahn, 16 September 2015, The United Methodist Church website, *umc.org/news-and-media/poll-small-changes-in-church-homosexuality-views.* Accessed 10 October 2016.
8. "United Methodists May Never Agree on LGBT Issues. Can They Stay Together Anyway?," by Michelle Boorstein, 9 May 2016, *The Washington Post* website, *tinyurl.com/zasa8yz.* Accessed 10 October 2016.

8 Final Thoughts

My heart was full of joy recently after I spent time meeting with a potential mentor. It is an indescribable privilege to serve alongside someone so excited to work with young people, someone who wants to help guide and encourage a confirmand on a journey to discover who God is and what God has for them. This man was so enthusiastic that his last words to me were, "Thank you for this opportunity. I can't wait to start! Being a mentor is going to be amazing!" How humbling to be able to work with such extraordinary servants.

While I am always eager to begin with a new group of confirmands, my heart is always amazed by and in awe of the mentors who give up so much of their time and energy to prepare young people for their faith journey ahead. My hope is that what is shared in this guide will be used to not only grow God's kingdom but also impact those serving to do so. Here are a few reminders:

- Play games and have fun with your young people!

- Be authentic. They will love you!

- Think of yourself as a guide, an encourager, friend, and a coach—all packaged into one!

- Confirmation is as much about the changing of one's heart as it is the changing of one's head.

- Each young person's confirmation journey will be as different and unique as he or she is.

- Confirmation should not be a viewed as a graduation but instead as a part of the discipleship process.

- **"All About Me!"** Have your young person fill out the All About Me form on page 82 of this guide and turn it in to you. This will provide great information to get to know the young person.

- **"Two Truths and a Lie."** Share three statements with your teenager, two that are true and one that is a lie. See if the teen can figure out which statement is the lie. Then switch and have the teen share three statements with you.

- **"House on Fire."** Ask your young person, If your house was on fire and there was time to grab only three items, what would the items be? Feel free to share what three things you would grab.

- **"Up and Down."** Ask your teen, Would you share the best thing that happened to you this week (your up) and the worst thing that happened to you (your down)? You can share some from your week as well.

- **"What If . . . ?"** Ask your teen "What if" questions and see what he or she says. The choices for this are endless. Some suggestions:

  —"What if you won the lottery? What would you do first?"

  —"What if you could go anywhere? Where would you go?"

  —"What if you could eat anything right now? What would it be?"

  —"What if you had one wish? What would it be?"

  —"What if you had more time in your day? How would you spend it?"

- **"Deserted Island."** Ask your teen, "If you were stranded on a deserted island and could eat only one food the whole time you were there, what would it be?"

- **"What's Next?"** Ask, What are three things you haven't tried but want to?

- **"Describe Me."** Ask the young person to share five words that would describe himself or herself.

- **"Baby Me."** Have each young person bring in a few baby/toddler pictures and share with one other.

My Life With Christ

Mark an "X" where you think you are now in each area.

How is:	Rarely	Sometimes	I Got This!
My reading and studying the Bible			
My desire to attend church			
My ability to be a part of my church			
My ability to forgive others			
My ability to forgive myself			
My concern to help others			
My desire to serve			
My hunger to see my friends come to know Jesus			
My ability to share my faith with others			
My desire to grow deeper in my own walk			

Confirmand's signature: _____

Date: _____

All About Me!

Name:

Nicknames:

Cell phone:

E-mail:

Birthday:

Family's names:

Favorite candy, cookie, or snack item:

Favorite TV show:

Favorite place to eat out:

Favorite color:

Hobbies/interests:

Areas of faith I would like to grow in:

Meeting Tracker

Confirmand: _____

Mentor: _____

Date	Location	Time Start	Time End	Summary and Comments

Meeting Tracker

Confirmand: _____

Mentor: _____

Date	Location	Time Start	Time End	Summary and Comments

My Mentors (for Mentor Reflection)

Who are the two or three people whom you consider your most trusted advisors in your life? How did they influence you positively and what qualities did they have that were important to you?

Name:

Influence:

Qualities:

My Mentors [for Mentor Reflection]

Who are the two or three people whom you consider your most trusted advisors in your life? How did they influence you positively and what qualities did they have that were important to you?

Name:

Influence:

Qualities:

My Mentors (for Mentor Reflection)

Who are the two or three people whom you consider your most trusted advisors in your life? How did they influence you positively and what qualities did they have that were important to you?

Name:

Influence:

Qualities:

Getting to Know Your Confirmands (1)

Confirmand name:

School:

How would you describe her or him?

Getting to Know Your Confirmands (1), continued

Who is her or his most important family relationships?

Who is his or her most important friend/peer relationships?

What is his or her favorite way to have fun?

What are her or his extracurricular activities?

My prayer for _____:

Getting to Know Your Confirmands (2)

Confirmand name:

School:

How would you describe her or him?

Getting to Know Your Confirmands (2), continued

Who is her or his most important family relationships?

Who is his or her most important friend/peer relationships?

What is his or her favorite way to have fun?

What are her or his extracurricular activities?

My prayer for _____:

Getting to Know Your Confirmands [3]

Confirmand name:

School:

How would you describe her or him?

Getting to Know Your Confirmands (3), continued

Who is her or his most important family relationships?

Who is his or her most important friend/peer relationships?

What is his or her favorite way to have fun?

What are her or his extracurricular activities?

My prayer for _____:

Getting to Know Your Confirmands (4)

Confirmand name:

School:

How would you describe her or him?

Getting to Know Your Confirmands (4), continued

Who is her or his most important family relationships?

Who is his or her most important friend/peer relationships?

What is his or her favorite way to have fun?

What are her or his extracurricular activities?

My prayer for _____:

Getting to Know Your Confirmands (5)

Confirmand name:

School:

How would you describe her or him?

Getting to Know Your Confirmands (5), continued

Who is her or his most important family relationships?

Who is his or her most important friend/peer relationships?

What is his or her favorite way to have fun?

What are her or his extracurricular activities?

My prayer for _____: